Seen walking our dog.
Plants.

The logbook is 6" x 9" and 120 Pages long to record your observations.

The dog's name is Tiddles and belongs to my best friends Jonathan and Julia Targett, whose walks, were the inspiration for this book. Also available two more logbooks:-
"Seen on walking our dog. Birds", and
"Seen on walking our dog. Insects".

As a logbook to record what you see or find, you will need another book on plants etc. to lookup for when you get home.

<table>
<tr><td colspan="6"><h1 align="center">Plants etc.</h1></td></tr>
<tr><td colspan="2">Vascular Plants (has flowers).</td><td colspan="2">Bryophytes (flowerless).</td><td colspan="2">Lichens (slow growing on rocks).</td></tr>
<tr><td>Grasses</td><td>☐</td><td>Mosses</td><td>☐</td><td>Lichens</td><td>☐</td></tr>
<tr><td>Sedges & Rushes</td><td>☐</td><td>Liverworts</td><td>☐</td><td></td><td></td></tr>
<tr><td>Trees</td><td>☐</td><td></td><td></td><td></td><td></td></tr>
<tr><td>Monocotyledons</td><td>☐</td><td></td><td></td><td></td><td></td></tr>
<tr><td>Dicotyledons</td><td>☐</td><td></td><td></td><td></td><td></td></tr>
<tr><td>Ferns</td><td>☐</td><td></td><td></td><td></td><td></td></tr>
<tr><td>Clubmosses</td><td>☐</td><td></td><td></td><td></td><td></td></tr>
</table>

Date: ___/___/___

Location: ____

Details: (Name)

Plants etc.

Vascular Plants (has flowers).		Bryophytes (flowerless).		Lichens (slow growing on rocks).	
Grasses	☐	Mosses	☐	Lichens	☐
Sedges & Rushes	☐	Liverworts	☐		
Trees	☐				
Monocotyledons	☐				
Dicotyledons	☐				
Ferns	☐				
Clubmosses	☐				

Date: ___/___/___

Location: ____________________________________

Details: (Name)

Plants etc.

Vascular Plants (has flowers).		Bryophytes (flowerless).		Lichens (slow growing on rocks).	
Grasses	☐	Mosses	☐	Lichens	☐
Sedges & Rushes	☐	Liverworts	☐		
Trees	☐				
Monocotyledons	☐				
Dicotyledons	☐				
Ferns	☐				
Clubmosses	☐				

Date: ___/___/___

Location: ____

Details: (Name)

Plants etc.

Vascular Plants (has flowers).		Bryophytes (flowerless).		Lichens (slow growing on rocks).	
Grasses	☐	Mosses	☐	Lichens	☐
Sedges & Rushes	☐	Liverworts	☐		
Trees	☐				
Monocotyledons	☐				
Dicotyledons	☐				
Ferns	☐				
Clubmosses	☐				

Date: ___/___/___

Location: ____

Details: (Name)

Plants etc.

Vascular Plants (has flowers).		Bryophytes (flowerless).		Lichens (slow growing on rocks).	
Grasses	☐	Mosses	☐	Lichens	☐
Sedges & Rushes	☐	Liverworts	☐		
Trees	☐				
Monocotyledons	☐				
Dicotyledons	☐				
Ferns	☐				
Clubmosses	☐				

Date: ___/___/___

Location: _______________________________________

Details: (Name)

Plants etc.

Vascular Plants (has flowers).		Bryophytes (flowerless).		Lichens (slow growing on rocks).	
Grasses	☐	Mosses	☐	Lichens	☐
Sedges & Rushes	☐	Liverworts	☐		
Trees	☐				
Monocotyledons	☐				
Dicotyledons	☐				
Ferns	☐				
Clubmosses	☐				

Date: ___/___/___

Location: ____

Details: (Name)

Plants etc.

Vascular Plants (has flowers).		Bryophytes (flowerless).		Lichens (slow growing on rocks).	
Grasses	☐	Mosses	☐	Lichens	☐
Sedges & Rushes	☐	Liverworts	☐		
Trees	☐				
Monocotyledons	☐				
Dicotyledons	☐				
Ferns	☐				
Clubmosses	☐				

Date: ___/___/___

Location: ____

Details: (Name)

Plants etc.

Vascular Plants (has flowers).		Bryophytes (flowerless).		Lichens (slow growing on rocks).	
Grasses	☐	Mosses	☐	Lichens	☐
Sedges & Rushes	☐	Liverworts	☐		
Trees	☐				
Monocotyledons	☐				
Dicotyledons	☐				
Ferns	☐				
Clubmosses	☐				

Date: ___/___/___

Location: ____

Details: (Name)

Plants etc.

Vascular Plants (has flowers).		Bryophytes (flowerless).		Lichens (slow growing on rocks).	
Grasses	☐	Mosses	☐	Lichens	☐
Sedges & Rushes	☐	Liverworts	☐		
Trees	☐				
Monocotyledons	☐				
Dicotyledons	☐				
Ferns	☐				
Clubmosses	☐				

Date: ___/___/___

Location: _______________________________________

Details: (Name)

Plants etc.

Vascular Plants (has flowers).		Bryophytes (flowerless).		Lichens (slow growing on rocks).	
Grasses	☐	Mosses	☐	Lichens	☐
Sedges & Rushes	☐	Liverworts	☐		
Trees	☐				
Monocotyledons	☐				
Dicotyledons	☐				
Ferns	☐				
Clubmosses	☐				

Date: ___/___/___

Location: ____

Details: (Name)

Plants etc.

Vascular Plants (has flowers).		Bryophytes (flowerless).		Lichens (slow growing on rocks).	
Grasses	☐	Mosses	☐	Lichens	☐
Sedges & Rushes	☐	Liverworts	☐		
Trees	☐				
Monocotyledons	☐				
Dicotyledons	☐				
Ferns	☐				
Clubmosses	☐				

Date: ___/___/___

Location: ____

Details: (Name)

Plants etc.

Vascular Plants (has flowers).		Bryophytes (flowerless).		Lichens (slow growing on rocks).	
Grasses	☐	Mosses	☐	Lichens	☐
Sedges & Rushes	☐	Liverworts	☐		
Trees	☐				
Monocotyledons	☐				
Dicotyledons	☐				
Ferns	☐				
Clubmosses	☐				

Date: ___/___/___

Location: ____

Details: (Name)

Plants etc.

Vascular Plants (has flowers).		Bryophytes (flowerless).		Lichens (slow growing on rocks).	
Grasses	☐	Mosses	☐	Lichens	☐
Sedges & Rushes	☐	Liverworts	☐		
Trees	☐				
Monocotyledons	☐				
Dicotyledons	☐				
Ferns	☐				
Clubmosses	☐				

Date: ___/___/___

Location: ____

Details: (Name)

Plants etc.

Vascular Plants (has flowers).		Bryophytes (flowerless).		Lichens (slow growing on rocks).	
Grasses	☐	Mosses	☐	Lichens	☐
Sedges & Rushes	☐	Liverworts	☐		
Trees	☐				
Monocotyledons	☐				
Dicotyledons	☐				
Ferns	☐				
Clubmosses	☐				

Date: ___/___/___

Location: ____

Details: (Name)

Plants etc.

Vascular Plants (has flowers).		Bryophytes (flowerless).		Lichens (slow growing on rocks).	
Grasses	☐	Mosses	☐	Lichens	☐
Sedges & Rushes	☐	Liverworts	☐		
Trees	☐				
Monocotyledons	☐				
Dicotyledons	☐				
Ferns	☐				
Clubmosses	☐				

Date: ___/___/___

Location: ____

Details: (Name)

Plants etc.

Vascular Plants (has flowers).		Bryophytes (flowerless).		Lichens (slow growing on rocks).	
Grasses	☐	Mosses	☐	Lichens	☐
Sedges & Rushes	☐	Liverworts	☐		
Trees	☐				
Monocotyledons	☐				
Dicotyledons	☐				
Ferns	☐				
Clubmosses	☐				

Date: ___/___/___

Location: ____

Details: (Name)

Plants etc.

Vascular Plants (has flowers).		Bryophytes (flowerless).		Lichens (slow growing on rocks).	
Grasses	☐	Mosses	☐	Lichens	☐
Sedges & Rushes	☐	Liverworts	☐		
Trees	☐				
Monocotyledons	☐				
Dicotyledons	☐				
Ferns	☐				
Clubmosses	☐				

Date: ___/___/___

Location: _______________________________________

Details: (Name)

Plants etc.

Vascular Plants (has flowers).		Bryophytes (flowerless).		Lichens (slow growing on rocks).	
Grasses	☐	Mosses	☐	Lichens	☐
Sedges & Rushes	☐	Liverworts	☐		
Trees	☐				
Monocotyledons	☐				
Dicotyledons	☐				
Ferns	☐				
Clubmosses	☐				

Date: ___/___/___

Location: ____

Details: (Name)

Plants etc.

Vascular Plants (has flowers).		Bryophytes (flowerless).		Lichens (slow growing on rocks).	
Grasses	☐	Mosses	☐	Lichens	☐
Sedges & Rushes	☐	Liverworts	☐		
Trees	☐				
Monocotyledons	☐				
Dicotyledons	☐				
Ferns	☐				
Clubmosses	☐				

Date: ___/___/___

Location: ____

Details: (Name)

Plants etc.

Vascular Plants (has flowers).		Bryophytes (flowerless).		Lichens (slow growing on rocks).	
Grasses	☐	Mosses	☐	Lichens	☐
Sedges & Rushes	☐	Liverworts	☐		
Trees	☐				
Monocotyledons	☐				
Dicotyledons	☐				
Ferns	☐				
Clubmosses	☐				

Date: ___/___/___

Location: _______________________________________

Details: (Name)

Plants etc.

Vascular Plants (has flowers).		Bryophytes (flowerless).		Lichens (slow growing on rocks).	
Grasses	☐	Mosses	☐	Lichens	☐
Sedges & Rushes	☐	Liverworts	☐		
Trees	☐				
Monocotyledons	☐				
Dicotyledons	☐				
Ferns	☐				
Clubmosses	☐				

Date: ___/___/___

Location: ____

Details: (Name)

Plants etc.

Vascular Plants (has flowers).		Bryophytes (flowerless).		Lichens (slow growing on rocks).	
Grasses	☐	Mosses	☐	Lichens	☐
Sedges & Rushes	☐	Liverworts	☐		
Trees	☐				
Monocotyledons	☐				
Dicotyledons	☐				
Ferns	☐				
Clubmosses	☐				

Date: ___/___/___

Location: ____

Details: (Name)

Plants etc.					
Vascular Plants (has flowers).		**Bryophytes (flowerless).**		**Lichens (slow growing on rocks).**	
Grasses	☐	Mosses	☐	Lichens	☐
Sedges & Rushes	☐	Liverworts	☐		
Trees	☐				
Monocotyledons	☐				
Dicotyledons	☐				
Ferns	☐				
Clubmosses	☐				

Date: ___/___/___

Location: ____

Details: (Name)

Plants etc.

Vascular Plants (has flowers).		Bryophytes (flowerless).		Lichens (slow growing on rocks).	
Grasses	☐	Mosses	☐	Lichens	☐
Sedges & Rushes	☐	Liverworts	☐		
Trees	☐				
Monocotyledons	☐				
Dicotyledons	☐				
Ferns	☐				
Clubmosses	☐				

Date: ___/___/___

Location: ____

Details: (Name)

Plants etc.

Vascular Plants (has flowers).		Bryophytes (flowerless).		Lichens (slow growing on rocks).	
Grasses	☐	Mosses	☐	Lichens	☐
Sedges & Rushes	☐	Liverworts	☐		
Trees	☐				
Monocotyledons	☐				
Dicotyledons	☐				
Ferns	☐				
Clubmosses	☐				

Date: ___/___/___

Location: ____

Details: (Name)

Plants etc.

Vascular Plants (has flowers).		Bryophytes (flowerless).		Lichens (slow growing on rocks).	
Grasses	☐	Mosses	☐	Lichens	☐
Sedges & Rushes	☐	Liverworts	☐		
Trees	☐				
Monocotyledons	☐				
Dicotyledons	☐				
Ferns	☐				
Clubmosses	☐				

Date: ___/___/___

Location: ____

Details: (Name)

Plants etc.

Vascular Plants (has flowers).		Bryophytes (flowerless).		Lichens (slow growing on rocks).	
Grasses	☐	Mosses	☐	Lichens	☐
Sedges & Rushes	☐	Liverworts	☐		
Trees	☐				
Monocotyledons	☐				
Dicotyledons	☐				
Ferns	☐				
Clubmosses	☐				

Date: ___/___/___

Location: ____

Details: (Name)

Plants etc.

Vascular Plants (has flowers).		Bryophytes (flowerless).		Lichens (slow growing on rocks).	
Grasses	☐	Mosses	☐	Lichens	☐
Sedges & Rushes	☐	Liverworts	☐		
Trees	☐				
Monocotyledons	☐				
Dicotyledons	☐				
Ferns	☐				
Clubmosses	☐				

Date: ___/___/___

Location: ____

Details: (Name)

Plants etc.

Vascular Plants (has flowers).		Bryophytes (flowerless).		Lichens (slow growing on rocks).	
Grasses	☐	Mosses	☐	Lichens	☐
Sedges & Rushes	☐	Liverworts	☐		
Trees	☐				
Monocotyledons	☐				
Dicotyledons	☐				
Ferns	☐				
Clubmosses	☐				

Date: ___/___/___

Location: ____

Details: (Name)

Plants etc.

Vascular Plants (has flowers).		Bryophytes (flowerless).		Lichens (slow growing on rocks).	
Grasses	☐	Mosses	☐	Lichens	☐
Sedges & Rushes	☐	Liverworts	☐		
Trees	☐				
Monocotyledons	☐				
Dicotyledons	☐				
Ferns	☐				
Clubmosses	☐				

Date: ___/___/___

Location: ____

Details: (Name)

Plants etc.

Vascular Plants (has flowers).		Bryophytes (flowerless).		Lichens (slow growing on rocks).	
Grasses	☐	Mosses	☐	Lichens	☐
Sedges & Rushes	☐	Liverworts	☐		
Trees	☐				
Monocotyledons	☐				
Dicotyledons	☐				
Ferns	☐				
Clubmosses	☐				

Date: ___/___/___

Location: ____

Details: (Name)

Plants etc.

Vascular Plants (has flowers).		Bryophytes (flowerless).		Lichens (slow growing on rocks).	
Grasses	☐	Mosses	☐	Lichens	☐
Sedges & Rushes	☐	Liverworts	☐		
Trees	☐				
Monocotyledons	☐				
Dicotyledons	☐				
Ferns	☐				
Clubmosses	☐				

Date: ___/___/___

Location: ____

Details: (Name)

Plants etc.

Vascular Plants (has flowers).		Bryophytes (flowerless).		Lichens (slow growing on rocks).	
Grasses	☐	Mosses	☐	Lichens	☐
Sedges & Rushes	☐	Liverworts	☐		
Trees	☐				
Monocotyledons	☐				
Dicotyledons	☐				
Ferns	☐				
Clubmosses	☐				

Date: ___/___/___

Location: ____

Details: (Name)

Plants etc.

Vascular Plants (has flowers).		Bryophytes (flowerless).		Lichens (slow growing on rocks).	
Grasses	☐	Mosses	☐	Lichens	☐
Sedges & Rushes	☐	Liverworts	☐		
Trees	☐				
Monocotyledons	☐				
Dicotyledons	☐				
Ferns	☐				
Clubmosses	☐				

Date: ___/___/___

Location: _______________________________________

Details: (Name)

Plants etc.

Vascular Plants (has flowers).		Bryophytes (flowerless).		Lichens (slow growing on rocks).	
Grasses	☐	Mosses	☐	Lichens	☐
Sedges & Rushes	☐	Liverworts	☐		
Trees	☐				
Monocotyledons	☐				
Dicotyledons	☐				
Ferns	☐				
Clubmosses	☐				

Date: ___/___/___

Location: ____

Details: (Name)

Plants etc.

Vascular Plants (has flowers).		Bryophytes (flowerless).		Lichens (slow growing on rocks).	
Grasses	☐	Mosses	☐	Lichens	☐
Sedges & Rushes	☐	Liverworts	☐		
Trees	☐				
Monocotyledons	☐				
Dicotyledons	☐				
Ferns	☐				
Clubmosses	☐				

Date: ___/___/___

Location: ____

Details: (Name)

Plants etc.

Vascular Plants (has flowers).		Bryophytes (flowerless).		Lichens (slow growing on rocks).	
Grasses	☐	Mosses	☐	Lichens	☐
Sedges & Rushes	☐	Liverworts	☐		
Trees	☐				
Monocotyledons	☐				
Dicotyledons	☐				
Ferns	☐				
Clubmosses	☐				

Date: ___/___/___

Location: ____

Details: (Name)

Plants etc.

Vascular Plants (has flowers).		Bryophytes (flowerless).		Lichens (slow growing on rocks).	
Grasses	☐	Mosses	☐	Lichens	☐
Sedges & Rushes	☐	Liverworts	☐		
Trees	☐				
Monocotyledons	☐				
Dicotyledons	☐				
Ferns	☐				
Clubmosses	☐				

Date: ___/___/___

Location: ____

Details: (Name)

Plants etc.

Vascular Plants (has flowers).		Bryophytes (flowerless).		Lichens (slow growing on rocks).	
Grasses	☐	Mosses	☐	Lichens	☐
Sedges & Rushes	☐	Liverworts	☐		
Trees	☐				
Monocotyledons	☐				
Dicotyledons	☐				
Ferns	☐				
Clubmosses	☐				

Date: ___/___/___

Location: ____

Details: (Name)

Plants etc.

Vascular Plants (has flowers).		Bryophytes (flowerless).		Lichens (slow growing on rocks).	
Grasses	☐	Mosses	☐	Lichens	☐
Sedges & Rushes	☐	Liverworts	☐		
Trees	☐				
Monocotyledons	☐				
Dicotyledons	☐				
Ferns	☐				
Clubmosses	☐				

Date: ___/___/___

Location: ____

Details: (Name)

Plants etc.

Vascular Plants (has flowers).		Bryophytes (flowerless).		Lichens (slow growing on rocks).	
Grasses	☐	Mosses	☐	Lichens	☐
Sedges & Rushes	☐	Liverworts	☐		
Trees	☐				
Monocotyledons	☐				
Dicotyledons	☐				
Ferns	☐				
Clubmosses	☐				

Date: ___/___/___

Location: ____

Details: (Name)

Plants etc.

Vascular Plants (has flowers).		Bryophytes (flowerless).		Lichens (slow growing on rocks).	
Grasses	☐	Mosses	☐	Lichens	☐
Sedges & Rushes	☐	Liverworts	☐		
Trees	☐				
Monocotyledons	☐				
Dicotyledons	☐				
Ferns	☐				
Clubmosses	☐				

Date: ___/___/___

Location: ____

Details: (Name)

Plants etc.

Vascular Plants (has flowers).		Bryophytes (flowerless).		Lichens (slow growing on rocks).	
Grasses	☐	Mosses	☐	Lichens	☐
Sedges & Rushes	☐	Liverworts	☐		
Trees	☐				
Monocotyledons	☐				
Dicotyledons	☐				
Ferns	☐				
Clubmosses	☐				

Date: ___/___/___

Location: ____

Details: (Name)

Plants etc.

Vascular Plants (has flowers).		Bryophytes (flowerless).		Lichens (slow growing on rocks).	
Grasses	☐	Mosses	☐	Lichens	☐
Sedges & Rushes	☐	Liverworts	☐		
Trees	☐				
Monocotyledons	☐				
Dicotyledons	☐				
Ferns	☐				
Clubmosses	☐				

Date: ___/___/___

Location: _______________________________________

Details: (Name)

Plants etc.

Vascular Plants (has flowers).		Bryophytes (flowerless).		Lichens (slow growing on rocks).	
Grasses	☐	Mosses	☐	Lichens	☐
Sedges & Rushes	☐	Liverworts	☐		
Trees	☐				
Monocotyledons	☐				
Dicotyledons	☐				
Ferns	☐				
Clubmosses	☐				

Date: ___/___/___

Location: ____

Details: (Name)

Plants etc.

Vascular Plants (has flowers).		Bryophytes (flowerless).		Lichens (slow growing on rocks).	
Grasses	☐	Mosses	☐	Lichens	☐
Sedges & Rushes	☐	Liverworts	☐		
Trees	☐				
Monocotyledons	☐				
Dicotyledons	☐				
Ferns	☐				
Clubmosses	☐				

Date: ___/___/___

Location: ____

Details: (Name)

Plants etc.

Vascular Plants (has flowers).		Bryophytes (flowerless).		Lichens (slow growing on rocks).	
Grasses	☐	Mosses	☐	Lichens	☐
Sedges & Rushes	☐	Liverworts	☐		
Trees	☐				
Monocotyledons	☐				
Dicotyledons	☐				
Ferns	☐				
Clubmosses	☐				

Date: ___/___/___

Location: ______________________________________

Details: (Name)

Plants etc.

Vascular Plants (has flowers).		Bryophytes (flowerless).		Lichens (slow growing on rocks).	
Grasses	☐	Mosses	☐	Lichens	☐
Sedges & Rushes	☐	Liverworts	☐		
Trees	☐				
Monocotyledons	☐				
Dicotyledons	☐				
Ferns	☐				
Clubmosses	☐				

Date: ___/___/___

Location: ____

Details: (Name)

Plants etc.

Vascular Plants (has flowers).		Bryophytes (flowerless).		Lichens (slow growing on rocks).	
Grasses	☐	Mosses	☐	Lichens	☐
Sedges & Rushes	☐	Liverworts	☐		
Trees	☐				
Monocotyledons	☐				
Dicotyledons	☐				
Ferns	☐				
Clubmosses	☐				

Date: ___/___/___

Location: ____

Details: (Name)

<table>
<tr><td colspan="6" align="center"># Plants etc.</td></tr>
<tr><td colspan="2">Vascular Plants (has flowers).</td><td colspan="2">Bryophytes (flowerless).</td><td colspan="2">Lichens (slow growing on rocks).</td></tr>
<tr><td>Grasses</td><td>☐</td><td>Mosses</td><td>☐</td><td>Lichens</td><td>☐</td></tr>
<tr><td>Sedges & Rushes</td><td>☐</td><td>Liverworts</td><td>☐</td><td></td><td></td></tr>
<tr><td>Trees</td><td>☐</td><td></td><td></td><td></td><td></td></tr>
<tr><td>Monocotyledons</td><td>☐</td><td></td><td></td><td></td><td></td></tr>
<tr><td>Dicotyledons</td><td>☐</td><td></td><td></td><td></td><td></td></tr>
<tr><td>Ferns</td><td>☐</td><td></td><td></td><td></td><td></td></tr>
<tr><td>Clubmosses</td><td>☐</td><td></td><td></td><td></td><td></td></tr>
</table>

Date: ___/___/___

Location: ___________________________________

Details: (Name)

Plants etc.

Vascular Plants (has flowers).		Bryophytes (flowerless).		Lichens (slow growing on rocks).	
Grasses	☐	Mosses	☐	Lichens	☐
Sedges & Rushes	☐	Liverworts	☐		
Trees	☐				
Monocotyledons	☐				
Dicotyledons	☐				
Ferns	☐				
Clubmosses	☐				

Date: ___/___/___

Location: ___________________________________

Details: (Name)

Plants etc.

Vascular Plants (has flowers).		Bryophytes (flowerless).		Lichens (slow growing on rocks).	
Grasses	☐	Mosses	☐	Lichens	☐
Sedges & Rushes	☐	Liverworts	☐		
Trees	☐				
Monocotyledons	☐				
Dicotyledons	☐				
Ferns	☐				
Clubmosses	☐				

Date: ___/___/___

Location: _______________________________________

Details: (Name)

Plants etc.

Vascular Plants (has flowers).		Bryophytes (flowerless).		Lichens (slow growing on rocks).	
Grasses	☐	Mosses	☐	Lichens	☐
Sedges & Rushes	☐	Liverworts	☐		
Trees	☐				
Monocotyledons	☐				
Dicotyledons	☐				
Ferns	☐				
Clubmosses	☐				

Date: ___/___/___

Location: ____

Details: (Name)

<table>
<tr><td colspan="6" align="center"><h1>Plants etc.</h1></td></tr>
<tr><td colspan="2">Vascular Plants (has flowers).</td><td colspan="2">Bryophytes (flowerless).</td><td colspan="2">Lichens (slow growing on rocks).</td></tr>
<tr><td>Grasses</td><td>☐</td><td>Mosses</td><td>☐</td><td>Lichens</td><td>☐</td></tr>
<tr><td>Sedges & Rushes</td><td>☐</td><td>Liverworts</td><td>☐</td><td></td><td></td></tr>
<tr><td>Trees</td><td>☐</td><td></td><td></td><td></td><td></td></tr>
<tr><td>Monocotyledons</td><td>☐</td><td></td><td></td><td></td><td></td></tr>
<tr><td>Dicotyledons</td><td>☐</td><td></td><td></td><td></td><td></td></tr>
<tr><td>Ferns</td><td>☐</td><td></td><td></td><td></td><td></td></tr>
<tr><td>Clubmosses</td><td>☐</td><td></td><td></td><td></td><td></td></tr>
</table>

Date: ___/___/___

Location: ____

Details: (Name)

Plants etc.

Vascular Plants (has flowers).		Bryophytes (flowerless).		Lichens (slow growing on rocks).	
Grasses	☐	Mosses	☐	Lichens	☐
Sedges & Rushes	☐	Liverworts	☐		
Trees	☐				
Monocotyledons	☐				
Dicotyledons	☐				
Ferns	☐				
Clubmosses	☐				

Date: ___/___/___

Location: _______________________________________

Details: (Name)

Plants etc.

Vascular Plants (has flowers).		Bryophytes (flowerless).		Lichens (slow growing on rocks).	
Grasses	☐	Mosses	☐	Lichens	☐
Sedges & Rushes	☐	Liverworts	☐		
Trees	☐				
Monocotyledons	☐				
Dicotyledons	☐				
Ferns	☐				
Clubmosses	☐				

Date: ___/___/___

Location: ______________________________________

Details: (Name)

Plants etc.

Vascular Plants (has flowers).		Bryophytes (flowerless).		Lichens (slow growing on rocks).	
Grasses	☐	Mosses	☐	Lichens	☐
Sedges & Rushes	☐	Liverworts	☐		
Trees	☐				
Monocotyledons	☐				
Dicotyledons	☐				
Ferns	☐				
Clubmosses	☐				

Date: ___/___/___

Location: ____

Details: (Name)

Plants etc.

Vascular Plants (has flowers).		Bryophytes (flowerless).		Lichens (slow growing on rocks).	
Grasses	☐	Mosses	☐	Lichens	☐
Sedges & Rushes	☐	Liverworts	☐		
Trees	☐				
Monocotyledons	☐				
Dicotyledons	☐				
Ferns	☐				
Clubmosses	☐				

Date: ___/___/___

Location: ______________________________________

Details: (Name)

Plants etc.

Vascular Plants (has flowers).		Bryophytes (flowerless).		Lichens (slow growing on rocks).	
Grasses	☐	Mosses	☐	Lichens	☐
Sedges & Rushes	☐	Liverworts	☐		
Trees	☐				
Monocotyledons	☐				
Dicotyledons	☐				
Ferns	☐				
Clubmosses	☐				

Date: ___/___/___

Location: ____

Details: (Name)

<table>
<tr><th colspan="6">Plants etc.</th></tr>
<tr><th colspan="2">Vascular Plants (has flowers).</th><th colspan="2">Bryophytes (flowerless).</th><th colspan="2">Lichens (slow growing on rocks).</th></tr>
<tr><td>Grasses</td><td>☐</td><td>Mosses</td><td>☐</td><td>Lichens</td><td>☐</td></tr>
<tr><td>Sedges & Rushes</td><td>☐</td><td>Liverworts</td><td>☐</td><td></td><td></td></tr>
<tr><td>Trees</td><td>☐</td><td></td><td></td><td></td><td></td></tr>
<tr><td>Monocotyledons</td><td>☐</td><td></td><td></td><td></td><td></td></tr>
<tr><td>Dicotyledons</td><td>☐</td><td></td><td></td><td></td><td></td></tr>
<tr><td>Ferns</td><td>☐</td><td></td><td></td><td></td><td></td></tr>
<tr><td>Clubmosses</td><td>☐</td><td></td><td></td><td></td><td></td></tr>
</table>

Date: ___/___/___

Location: ____

Details: (Name)

Plants etc.

Vascular Plants (has flowers).		Bryophytes (flowerless).		Lichens (slow growing on rocks).	
Grasses	☐	Mosses	☐	Lichens	☐
Sedges & Rushes	☐	Liverworts	☐		
Trees	☐				
Monocotyledons	☐				
Dicotyledons	☐				
Ferns	☐				
Clubmosses	☐				

Date: ___/___/___

Location: ____

Details: (Name)

Plants etc.

Vascular Plants (has flowers).		Bryophytes (flowerless).		Lichens (slow growing on rocks).	
Grasses	☐	Mosses	☐	Lichens	☐
Sedges & Rushes	☐	Liverworts	☐		
Trees	☐				
Monocotyledons	☐				
Dicotyledons	☐				
Ferns	☐				
Clubmosses	☐				

Date: ___/___/___

Location: ____

Details: (Name)

Plants etc.

Vascular Plants (has flowers).		Bryophytes (flowerless).		Lichens (slow growing on rocks).	
Grasses	☐	Mosses	☐	Lichens	☐
Sedges & Rushes	☐	Liverworts	☐		
Trees	☐				
Monocotyledons	☐				
Dicotyledons	☐				
Ferns	☐				
Clubmosses	☐				

Date: ___/___/___

Location: ____

Details: (Name)

<table>
<tr><td colspan="6" align="center">Plants etc.</td></tr>
<tr><td colspan="2">Vascular Plants (has flowers).</td><td colspan="2">Bryophytes (flowerless).</td><td colspan="2">Lichens (slow growing on rocks).</td></tr>
<tr><td>Grasses</td><td>☐</td><td>Mosses</td><td>☐</td><td>Lichens</td><td>☐</td></tr>
<tr><td>Sedges & Rushes</td><td>☐</td><td>Liverworts</td><td>☐</td><td></td><td></td></tr>
<tr><td>Trees</td><td>☐</td><td></td><td></td><td></td><td></td></tr>
<tr><td>Monocotyledons</td><td>☐</td><td></td><td></td><td></td><td></td></tr>
<tr><td>Dicotyledons</td><td>☐</td><td></td><td></td><td></td><td></td></tr>
<tr><td>Ferns</td><td>☐</td><td></td><td></td><td></td><td></td></tr>
<tr><td>Clubmosses</td><td>☐</td><td></td><td></td><td></td><td></td></tr>
</table>

Date: ___/___/___

Location: ____

Details: (Name)

Plants etc.

Vascular Plants (has flowers).		Bryophytes (flowerless).		Lichens (slow growing on rocks).	
Grasses	☐	Mosses	☐	Lichens	☐
Sedges & Rushes	☐	Liverworts	☐		
Trees	☐				
Monocotyledons	☐				
Dicotyledons	☐				
Ferns	☐				
Clubmosses	☐				

Date: ___/___/___

Location: ____

Details: (Name)

Plants etc.

Vascular Plants (has flowers).		Bryophytes (flowerless).		Lichens (slow growing on rocks).	
Grasses	☐	Mosses	☐	Lichens	☐
Sedges & Rushes	☐	Liverworts	☐		
Trees	☐				
Monocotyledons	☐				
Dicotyledons	☐				
Ferns	☐				
Clubmosses	☐				

Date: ___/___/___

Location: ____

Details: (Name)

Plants etc.

Vascular Plants (has flowers).		Bryophytes (flowerless).		Lichens (slow growing on rocks).	
Grasses	☐	Mosses	☐	Lichens	☐
Sedges & Rushes	☐	Liverworts	☐		
Trees	☐				
Monocotyledons	☐				
Dicotyledons	☐				
Ferns	☐				
Clubmosses	☐				

Date: ___/___/___

Location: ____

Details: (Name)

Plants etc.

Vascular Plants (has flowers).		Bryophytes (flowerless).		Lichens (slow growing on rocks).	
Grasses	☐	Mosses	☐	Lichens	☐
Sedges & Rushes	☐	Liverworts	☐		
Trees	☐				
Monocotyledons	☐				
Dicotyledons	☐				
Ferns	☐				
Clubmosses	☐				

Date: ___/___/___

Location: ____

Details: (Name)

<table>
<tr><td colspan="6" align="center">Plants etc.</td></tr>
<tr>
<td colspan="2">Vascular Plants (has flowers).</td>
<td colspan="2">Bryophytes (flowerless).</td>
<td colspan="2">Lichens (slow growing on rocks).</td>
</tr>
<tr><td>Grasses</td><td>☐</td><td>Mosses</td><td>☐</td><td>Lichens</td><td>☐</td></tr>
<tr><td>Sedges & Rushes</td><td>☐</td><td>Liverworts</td><td>☐</td><td></td><td></td></tr>
<tr><td>Trees</td><td>☐</td><td></td><td></td><td></td><td></td></tr>
<tr><td>Monocotyledons</td><td>☐</td><td></td><td></td><td></td><td></td></tr>
<tr><td>Dicotyledons</td><td>☐</td><td></td><td></td><td></td><td></td></tr>
<tr><td>Ferns</td><td>☐</td><td></td><td></td><td></td><td></td></tr>
<tr><td>Clubmosses</td><td>☐</td><td></td><td></td><td></td><td></td></tr>
</table>

Date: ___/___/___

Location: ____

Details: (Name)

Plants etc.

Vascular Plants (has flowers).		Bryophytes (flowerless).		Lichens (slow growing on rocks).	
Grasses	☐	Mosses	☐	Lichens	☐
Sedges & Rushes	☐	Liverworts	☐		
Trees	☐				
Monocotyledons	☐				
Dicotyledons	☐				
Ferns	☐				
Clubmosses	☐				

Date: ___/___/___

Location: ____

Details: (Name)

Plants etc.

Vascular Plants (has flowers).		Bryophytes (flowerless).		Lichens (slow growing on rocks).	
Grasses	☐	Mosses	☐	Lichens	☐
Sedges & Rushes	☐	Liverworts	☐		
Trees	☐				
Monocotyledons	☐				
Dicotyledons	☐				
Ferns	☐				
Clubmosses	☐				

Date: ___/___/___

Location: ____

Details: (Name)

Plants etc.

Vascular Plants (has flowers).		Bryophytes (flowerless).		Lichens (slow growing on rocks).	
Grasses	☐	Mosses	☐	Lichens	☐
Sedges & Rushes	☐	Liverworts	☐		
Trees	☐				
Monocotyledons	☐				
Dicotyledons	☐				
Ferns	☐				
Clubmosses	☐				

Date: ___/___/___

Location: ____

Details: (Name)

Plants etc.

Vascular Plants (has flowers).		Bryophytes (flowerless).		Lichens (slow growing on rocks).	
Grasses	☐	Mosses	☐	Lichens	☐
Sedges & Rushes	☐	Liverworts	☐		
Trees	☐				
Monocotyledons	☐				
Dicotyledons	☐				
Ferns	☐				
Clubmosses	☐				

Date: ___/___/___

Location: ____

Details: (Name)

Plants etc.

Vascular Plants (has flowers).		Bryophytes (flowerless).		Lichens (slow growing on rocks).	
Grasses	☐	Mosses	☐	Lichens	☐
Sedges & Rushes	☐	Liverworts	☐		
Trees	☐				
Monocotyledons	☐				
Dicotyledons	☐				
Ferns	☐				
Clubmosses	☐				

Date: ___/___/___

Location: ____

Details: (Name)

Plants etc.

Vascular Plants (has flowers).		Bryophytes (flowerless).		Lichens (slow growing on rocks).	
Grasses	☐	Mosses	☐	Lichens	☐
Sedges & Rushes	☐	Liverworts	☐		
Trees	☐				
Monocotyledons	☐				
Dicotyledons	☐				
Ferns	☐				
Clubmosses	☐				

Date: ___/___/___

Location: ____

Details: (Name)

Plants etc.

Vascular Plants (has flowers).		Bryophytes (flowerless).		Lichens (slow growing on rocks).	
Grasses	☐	Mosses	☐	Lichens	☐
Sedges & Rushes	☐	Liverworts	☐		
Trees	☐				
Monocotyledons	☐				
Dicotyledons	☐				
Ferns	☐				
Clubmosses	☐				

Date: ___/___/___

Location: ____

Details: (Name)

<table>
<tr><td colspan="6" align="center">Plants etc.</td></tr>
<tr><td colspan="2">Vascular Plants (has flowers).</td><td colspan="2">Bryophytes (flowerless).</td><td colspan="2">Lichens (slow growing on rocks).</td></tr>
<tr><td>Grasses</td><td>☐</td><td>Mosses</td><td>☐</td><td>Lichens</td><td>☐</td></tr>
<tr><td>Sedges & Rushes</td><td>☐</td><td>Liverworts</td><td>☐</td><td></td><td></td></tr>
<tr><td>Trees</td><td>☐</td><td></td><td></td><td></td><td></td></tr>
<tr><td>Monocotyledons</td><td>☐</td><td></td><td></td><td></td><td></td></tr>
<tr><td>Dicotyledons</td><td>☐</td><td></td><td></td><td></td><td></td></tr>
<tr><td>Ferns</td><td>☐</td><td></td><td></td><td></td><td></td></tr>
<tr><td>Clubmosses</td><td>☐</td><td></td><td></td><td></td><td></td></tr>
</table>

Date: ___/___/___

Location: ___________________________________

Details: (Name)

Plants etc.

Vascular Plants (has flowers).		Bryophytes (flowerless).		Lichens (slow growing on rocks).	
Grasses	☐	Mosses	☐	Lichens	☐
Sedges & Rushes	☐	Liverworts	☐		
Trees	☐				
Monocotyledons	☐				
Dicotyledons	☐				
Ferns	☐				
Clubmosses	☐				

Date: ___/___/___

Location: ____

Details: (Name)

Plants etc.

Vascular Plants (has flowers).		Bryophytes (flowerless).		Lichens (slow growing on rocks).	
Grasses	☐	Mosses	☐	Lichens	☐
Sedges & Rushes	☐	Liverworts	☐		
Trees	☐				
Monocotyledons	☐				
Dicotyledons	☐				
Ferns	☐				
Clubmosses	☐				

Date: ___/___/___

Location: ____

Details: (Name)

Plants etc.

Vascular Plants (has flowers).		Bryophytes (flowerless).		Lichens (slow growing on rocks).	
Grasses	☐	Mosses	☐	Lichens	☐
Sedges & Rushes	☐	Liverworts	☐		
Trees	☐				
Monocotyledons	☐				
Dicotyledons	☐				
Ferns	☐				
Clubmosses	☐				

Date: ___/___/___

Location: ____

Details: (Name)

Plants etc.

Vascular Plants (has flowers).		Bryophytes (flowerless).		Lichens (slow growing on rocks).	
Grasses	☐	Mosses	☐	Lichens	☐
Sedges & Rushes	☐	Liverworts	☐		
Trees	☐				
Monocotyledons	☐				
Dicotyledons	☐				
Ferns	☐				
Clubmosses	☐				

Date: ___/___/___

Location: ____

Details: (Name)

Plants etc.

Vascular Plants (has flowers).		Bryophytes (flowerless).		Lichens (slow growing on rocks).	
Grasses	☐	Mosses	☐	Lichens	☐
Sedges & Rushes	☐	Liverworts	☐		
Trees	☐				
Monocotyledons	☐				
Dicotyledons	☐				
Ferns	☐				
Clubmosses	☐				

Date: ___/___/___

Location: ____

Details: (Name)

Plants etc.

Vascular Plants (has flowers).		Bryophytes (flowerless).		Lichens (slow growing on rocks).	
Grasses	☐	Mosses	☐	Lichens	☐
Sedges & Rushes	☐	Liverworts	☐		
Trees	☐				
Monocotyledons	☐				
Dicotyledons	☐				
Ferns	☐				
Clubmosses	☐				

Date: ___/___/___

Location: _______________________________________

Details: (Name)

<table>
<tr><td colspan="6" align="center"><h2>Plants etc.</h2></td></tr>
<tr>
<td colspan="2">Vascular Plants (has flowers).</td>
<td colspan="2">Bryophytes (flowerless).</td>
<td colspan="2">Lichens (slow growing on rocks).</td>
</tr>
<tr><td>Grasses</td><td>☐</td><td>Mosses</td><td>☐</td><td>Lichens</td><td>☐</td></tr>
<tr><td>Sedges & Rushes</td><td>☐</td><td>Liverworts</td><td>☐</td><td></td><td></td></tr>
<tr><td>Trees</td><td>☐</td><td></td><td></td><td></td><td></td></tr>
<tr><td>Monocotyledons</td><td>☐</td><td></td><td></td><td></td><td></td></tr>
<tr><td>Dicotyledons</td><td>☐</td><td></td><td></td><td></td><td></td></tr>
<tr><td>Ferns</td><td>☐</td><td></td><td></td><td></td><td></td></tr>
<tr><td>Clubmosses</td><td>☐</td><td></td><td></td><td></td><td></td></tr>
</table>

Date: ___/___/___

Location: ____

Details: (Name)

Plants etc.

Vascular Plants (has flowers).		Bryophytes (flowerless).		Lichens (slow growing on rocks).	
Grasses	☐	Mosses	☐	Lichens	☐
Sedges & Rushes	☐	Liverworts	☐		
Trees	☐				
Monocotyledons	☐				
Dicotyledons	☐				
Ferns	☐				
Clubmosses	☐				

Date: ___/___/___

Location: ____

Details: (Name)

Plants etc.

Vascular Plants (has flowers).		Bryophytes (flowerless).		Lichens (slow growing on rocks).	
Grasses	☐	Mosses	☐	Lichens	☐
Sedges & Rushes	☐	Liverworts	☐		
Trees	☐				
Monocotyledons	☐				
Dicotyledons	☐				
Ferns	☐				
Clubmosses	☐				

Date: ___/___/___

Location: ____

Details: (Name)

Plants etc.

Vascular Plants (has flowers).		Bryophytes (flowerless).		Lichens (slow growing on rocks).	
Grasses	☐	Mosses	☐	Lichens	☐
Sedges & Rushes	☐	Liverworts	☐		
Trees	☐				
Monocotyledons	☐				
Dicotyledons	☐				
Ferns	☐				
Clubmosses	☐				

Date: ___/___/___

Location: ____

Details: (Name)

Plants etc.

Vascular Plants (has flowers).		Bryophytes (flowerless).		Lichens (slow growing on rocks).	
Grasses	☐	Mosses	☐	Lichens	☐
Sedges & Rushes	☐	Liverworts	☐		
Trees	☐				
Monocotyledons	☐				
Dicotyledons	☐				
Ferns	☐				
Clubmosses	☐				

Date: ___/___/___

Location: ____

Details: (Name)

Plants etc.

Vascular Plants (has flowers).		Bryophytes (flowerless).		Lichens (slow growing on rocks).	
Grasses	☐	Mosses	☐	Lichens	☐
Sedges & Rushes	☐	Liverworts	☐		
Trees	☐				
Monocotyledons	☐				
Dicotyledons	☐				
Ferns	☐				
Clubmosses	☐				

Date: ___/___/___

Location: ____

Details: (Name)

Plants etc.

Vascular Plants (has flowers).		Bryophytes (flowerless).		Lichens (slow growing on rocks).	
Grasses	☐	Mosses	☐	Lichens	☐
Sedges & Rushes	☐	Liverworts	☐		
Trees	☐				
Monocotyledons	☐				
Dicotyledons	☐				
Ferns	☐				
Clubmosses	☐				

Date: ___/___/___

Location: ____

Details: (Name)

Plants etc.

Vascular Plants (has flowers).		Bryophytes (flowerless).		Lichens (slow growing on rocks).	
Grasses	☐	Mosses	☐	Lichens	☐
Sedges & Rushes	☐	Liverworts	☐		
Trees	☐				
Monocotyledons	☐				
Dicotyledons	☐				
Ferns	☐				
Clubmosses	☐				

Date: ___/___/___

Location: ____

Details: (Name)

Plants etc.

Vascular Plants (has flowers).		Bryophytes (flowerless).		Lichens (slow growing on rocks).	
Grasses	☐	Mosses	☐	Lichens	☐
Sedges & Rushes	☐	Liverworts	☐		
Trees	☐				
Monocotyledons	☐				
Dicotyledons	☐				
Ferns	☐				
Clubmosses	☐				

Date: ___/___/___

Location: ____

Details: (Name)

Plants etc.

Vascular Plants (has flowers).		Bryophytes (flowerless).		Lichens (slow growing on rocks).	
Grasses	☐	Mosses	☐	Lichens	☐
Sedges & Rushes	☐	Liverworts	☐		
Trees	☐				
Monocotyledons	☐				
Dicotyledons	☐				
Ferns	☐				
Clubmosses	☐				

Date: ___/___/___

Location: ____

Details: (Name)

Plants etc.

Vascular Plants (has flowers).		Bryophytes (flowerless).		Lichens (slow growing on rocks).	
Grasses	☐	Mosses	☐	Lichens	☐
Sedges & Rushes	☐	Liverworts	☐		
Trees	☐				
Monocotyledons	☐				
Dicotyledons	☐				
Ferns	☐				
Clubmosses	☐				

Date: ___/___/___

Location: _______________________________________

Details: (Name)

Plants etc.

Vascular Plants (has flowers).		Bryophytes (flowerless).		Lichens (slow growing on rocks).	
Grasses	☐	Mosses	☐	Lichens	☐
Sedges & Rushes	☐	Liverworts	☐		
Trees	☐				
Monocotyledons	☐				
Dicotyledons	☐				
Ferns	☐				
Clubmosses	☐				

Date: ___/___/___

Location: ____

Details: (Name)

<table>
<tr><th colspan="6" align="center"><h1>Plants etc.</h1></th></tr>
<tr>
<th colspan="2">Vascular Plants (has flowers).</th>
<th colspan="2">Bryophytes (flowerless).</th>
<th colspan="2">Lichens (slow growing on rocks).</th>
</tr>
<tr><td>Grasses</td><td>☐</td><td>Mosses</td><td>☐</td><td>Lichens</td><td>☐</td></tr>
<tr><td>Sedges & Rushes</td><td>☐</td><td>Liverworts</td><td>☐</td><td></td><td></td></tr>
<tr><td>Trees</td><td>☐</td><td></td><td></td><td></td><td></td></tr>
<tr><td>Monocotyledons</td><td>☐</td><td></td><td></td><td></td><td></td></tr>
<tr><td>Dicotyledons</td><td>☐</td><td></td><td></td><td></td><td></td></tr>
<tr><td>Ferns</td><td>☐</td><td></td><td></td><td></td><td></td></tr>
<tr><td>Clubmosses</td><td>☐</td><td></td><td></td><td></td><td></td></tr>
</table>

Date: ___/___/___

Location: ____

Details: (Name)

Plants etc.

Vascular Plants (has flowers).		Bryophytes (flowerless).		Lichens (slow growing on rocks).	
Grasses	☐	Mosses	☐	Lichens	☐
Sedges & Rushes	☐	Liverworts	☐		
Trees	☐				
Monocotyledons	☐				
Dicotyledons	☐				
Ferns	☐				
Clubmosses	☐				

Date: ___/___/___

Location: ____

Details: (Name)

Plants etc.

Vascular Plants (has flowers).		Bryophytes (flowerless).		Lichens (slow growing on rocks).	
Grasses	☐	Mosses	☐	Lichens	☐
Sedges & Rushes	☐	Liverworts	☐		
Trees	☐				
Monocotyledons	☐				
Dicotyledons	☐				
Ferns	☐				
Clubmosses	☐				

Date: ___/___/___

Location: ______________________________________

Details: (Name)

<table>
<tr><th colspan="6" style="text-align:center">Plants etc.</th></tr>
<tr><th colspan="2">Vascular Plants (has flowers).</th><th colspan="2">Bryophytes (flowerless).</th><th colspan="2">Lichens (slow growing on rocks).</th></tr>
<tr><td>Grasses</td><td>☐</td><td>Mosses</td><td>☐</td><td>Lichens</td><td>☐</td></tr>
<tr><td>Sedges & Rushes</td><td>☐</td><td>Liverworts</td><td>☐</td><td></td><td></td></tr>
<tr><td>Trees</td><td>☐</td><td></td><td></td><td></td><td></td></tr>
<tr><td>Monocotyledons</td><td>☐</td><td></td><td></td><td></td><td></td></tr>
<tr><td>Dicotyledons</td><td>☐</td><td></td><td></td><td></td><td></td></tr>
<tr><td>Ferns</td><td>☐</td><td></td><td></td><td></td><td></td></tr>
<tr><td>Clubmosses</td><td>☐</td><td></td><td></td><td></td><td></td></tr>
</table>

Date: ___/___/___

Location: ____________________________________

Details: (Name)

Plants etc.

Vascular Plants (has flowers).		Bryophytes (flowerless).		Lichens (slow growing on rocks).	
Grasses	☐	Mosses	☐	Lichens	☐
Sedges & Rushes	☐	Liverworts	☐		
Trees	☐				
Monocotyledons	☐				
Dicotyledons	☐				
Ferns	☐				
Clubmosses	☐				

Date: ___/___/___

Location: ____

Details: (Name)

Plants etc.

Vascular Plants (has flowers).		Bryophytes (flowerless).		Lichens (slow growing on rocks).	
Grasses	☐	Mosses	☐	Lichens	☐
Sedges & Rushes	☐	Liverworts	☐		
Trees	☐				
Monocotyledons	☐				
Dicotyledons	☐				
Ferns	☐				
Clubmosses	☐				

Date: ___/___/___

Location: ____

Details: (Name)

<table>
<tr><td colspan="6"><h2 align="center">Plants etc.</h2></td></tr>
<tr><td colspan="2">Vascular Plants (has flowers).</td><td colspan="2">Bryophytes (flowerless).</td><td colspan="2">Lichens (slow growing on rocks).</td></tr>
<tr><td>Grasses</td><td>☐</td><td>Mosses</td><td>☐</td><td>Lichens</td><td>☐</td></tr>
<tr><td>Sedges & Rushes</td><td>☐</td><td>Liverworts</td><td>☐</td><td></td><td></td></tr>
<tr><td>Trees</td><td>☐</td><td></td><td></td><td></td><td></td></tr>
<tr><td>Monocotyledons</td><td>☐</td><td></td><td></td><td></td><td></td></tr>
<tr><td>Dicotyledons</td><td>☐</td><td></td><td></td><td></td><td></td></tr>
<tr><td>Ferns</td><td>☐</td><td></td><td></td><td></td><td></td></tr>
<tr><td>Clubmosses</td><td>☐</td><td></td><td></td><td></td><td></td></tr>
</table>

Date: ___/___/___

Location: ____

Details: (Name)

Plants etc.

Vascular Plants (has flowers).		Bryophytes (flowerless).		Lichens (slow growing on rocks).	
Grasses	☐	Mosses	☐	Lichens	☐
Sedges & Rushes	☐	Liverworts	☐		
Trees	☐				
Monocotyledons	☐				
Dicotyledons	☐				
Ferns	☐				
Clubmosses	☐				

Date: ___/___/___

Location: ____

Details: (Name)

Plants etc.

Vascular Plants (has flowers).		Bryophytes (flowerless).		Lichens (slow growing on rocks).	
Grasses	☐	Mosses	☐	Lichens	☐
Sedges & Rushes	☐	Liverworts	☐		
Trees	☐				
Monocotyledons	☐				
Dicotyledons	☐				
Ferns	☐				
Clubmosses	☐				

Date: ___/___/___

Location: ____

Details: (Name)

Plants etc.

Vascular Plants (has flowers).		Bryophytes (flowerless).		Lichens (slow growing on rocks).	
Grasses	☐	Mosses	☐	Lichens	☐
Sedges & Rushes	☐	Liverworts	☐		
Trees	☐				
Monocotyledons	☐				
Dicotyledons	☐				
Ferns	☐				
Clubmosses	☐				

Date: ___/___/___

Location: ____

Details: (Name)

Plants etc.

Vascular Plants (has flowers).		Bryophytes (flowerless).		Lichens (slow growing on rocks).	
Grasses	☐	Mosses	☐	Lichens	☐
Sedges & Rushes	☐	Liverworts	☐		
Trees	☐				
Monocotyledons	☐				
Dicotyledons	☐				
Ferns	☐				
Clubmosses	☐				

Date: ___/___/___

Location: ____

Details: (Name)

Plants etc.

Vascular Plants (has flowers).		Bryophytes (flowerless).		Lichens (slow growing on rocks).	
Grasses	☐	Mosses	☐	Lichens	☐
Sedges & Rushes	☐	Liverworts	☐		
Trees	☐				
Monocotyledons	☐				
Dicotyledons	☐				
Ferns	☐				
Clubmosses	☐				

Date: ___/___/___

Location: ____

Details: (Name)

Plants etc.

Vascular Plants (has flowers).		Bryophytes (flowerless).		Lichens (slow growing on rocks).	
Grasses	☐	Mosses	☐	Lichens	☐
Sedges & Rushes	☐	Liverworts	☐		
Trees	☐				
Monocotyledons	☐				
Dicotyledons	☐				
Ferns	☐				
Clubmosses	☐				

Date: ___/___/___

Location: ____

Details: (Name)

Plants etc.

Vascular Plants (has flowers).		Bryophytes (flowerless).		Lichens (slow growing on rocks).	
Grasses	☐	Mosses	☐	Lichens	☐
Sedges & Rushes	☐	Liverworts	☐		
Trees	☐				
Monocotyledons	☐				
Dicotyledons	☐				
Ferns	☐				
Clubmosses	☐				

Date: ___/___/___

Location: ____

Details: (Name)

Plants etc.

Vascular Plants (has flowers).		Bryophytes (flowerless).		Lichens (slow growing on rocks).	
Grasses	☐	Mosses	☐	Lichens	☐
Sedges & Rushes	☐	Liverworts	☐		
Trees	☐				
Monocotyledons	☐				
Dicotyledons	☐				
Ferns	☐				
Clubmosses	☐				

Date: ___/___/___

Location: ____

Details: (Name)

Plants etc.

Vascular Plants (has flowers).		Bryophytes (flowerless).		Lichens (slow growing on rocks).	
Grasses	☐	Mosses	☐	Lichens	☐
Sedges & Rushes	☐	Liverworts	☐		
Trees	☐				
Monocotyledons	☐				
Dicotyledons	☐				
Ferns	☐				
Clubmosses	☐				

Date: ___/___/___

Location: ____

Details: (Name)

Plants etc.

Vascular Plants (has flowers).		Bryophytes (flowerless).		Lichens (slow growing on rocks).	
Grasses	☐	Mosses	☐	Lichens	☐
Sedges & Rushes	☐	Liverworts	☐		
Trees	☐				
Monocotyledons	☐				
Dicotyledons	☐				
Ferns	☐				
Clubmosses	☐				

Date: ___/___/___

Location: ____

Details: (Name)

Plants etc.

Vascular Plants (has flowers).		Bryophytes (flowerless).		Lichens (slow growing on rocks).	
Grasses	☐	Mosses	☐	Lichens	☐
Sedges & Rushes	☐	Liverworts	☐		
Trees	☐				
Monocotyledons	☐				
Dicotyledons	☐				
Ferns	☐				
Clubmosses	☐				

Date: ___/___/___

Location: ____

Details: (Name)

<table>
<tr><td colspan="6"><h1 align="center">Plants etc.</h1></td></tr>
<tr><td colspan="2">Vascular Plants (has flowers).</td><td colspan="2">Bryophytes (flowerless).</td><td colspan="2">Lichens (slow growing on rocks).</td></tr>
<tr><td>Grasses</td><td>☐</td><td>Mosses</td><td>☐</td><td>Lichens</td><td>☐</td></tr>
<tr><td>Sedges & Rushes</td><td>☐</td><td>Liverworts</td><td>☐</td><td></td><td></td></tr>
<tr><td>Trees</td><td>☐</td><td></td><td></td><td></td><td></td></tr>
<tr><td>Monocotyledons</td><td>☐</td><td></td><td></td><td></td><td></td></tr>
<tr><td>Dicotyledons</td><td>☐</td><td></td><td></td><td></td><td></td></tr>
<tr><td>Ferns</td><td>☐</td><td></td><td></td><td></td><td></td></tr>
<tr><td>Clubmosses</td><td>☐</td><td></td><td></td><td></td><td></td></tr>
</table>

Date: ___/___/___

Location: ____

Details: (Name)

Plants etc.

Vascular Plants (has flowers).		Bryophytes (flowerless).		Lichens (slow growing on rocks).	
Grasses	☐	Mosses	☐	Lichens	☐
Sedges & Rushes	☐	Liverworts	☐		
Trees	☐				
Monocotyledons	☐				
Dicotyledons	☐				
Ferns	☐				
Clubmosses	☐				

Date: ___/___/___

Location: ____

Details: (Name)

<table>
<tr><td colspan="6" align="center"><h1>Plants etc.</h1></td></tr>
<tr><td colspan="2">Vascular Plants (has flowers).</td><td colspan="2">Bryophytes (flowerless).</td><td colspan="2">Lichens (slow growing on rocks).</td></tr>
<tr><td>Grasses</td><td>☐</td><td>Mosses</td><td>☐</td><td>Lichens</td><td>☐</td></tr>
<tr><td>Sedges & Rushes</td><td>☐</td><td>Liverworts</td><td>☐</td><td></td><td></td></tr>
<tr><td>Trees</td><td>☐</td><td></td><td></td><td></td><td></td></tr>
<tr><td>Monocotyledons</td><td>☐</td><td></td><td></td><td></td><td></td></tr>
<tr><td>Dicotyledons</td><td>☐</td><td></td><td></td><td></td><td></td></tr>
<tr><td>Ferns</td><td>☐</td><td></td><td></td><td></td><td></td></tr>
<tr><td>Clubmosses</td><td>☐</td><td></td><td></td><td></td><td></td></tr>
</table>

Date: ___/___/___

Location: ____

Details: (Name)

Plants etc.

Vascular Plants (has flowers).		Bryophytes (flowerless).		Lichens (slow growing on rocks).	
Grasses	☐	Mosses	☐	Lichens	☐
Sedges & Rushes	☐	Liverworts	☐		
Trees	☐				
Monocotyledons	☐				
Dicotyledons	☐				
Ferns	☐				
Clubmosses	☐				

Date: ___/___/___

Location: ____

Details: (Name)

Plants etc.

Vascular Plants (has flowers).		Bryophytes (flowerless).		Lichens (slow growing on rocks).	
Grasses	☐	Mosses	☐	Lichens	☐
Sedges & Rushes	☐	Liverworts	☐		
Trees	☐				
Monocotyledons	☐				
Dicotyledons	☐				
Ferns	☐				
Clubmosses	☐				

Date: ___/___/___

Location: ____

Details: (Name)

Plants etc.

Vascular Plants (has flowers).		Bryophytes (flowerless).		Lichens (slow growing on rocks).	
Grasses	☐	Mosses	☐	Lichens	☐
Sedges & Rushes	☐	Liverworts	☐		
Trees	☐				
Monocotyledons	☐				
Dicotyledons	☐				
Ferns	☐				
Clubmosses	☐				

Date: ___/___/___

Location: ____

Details: (Name)